The Comedians Trivia Book II

ALSO BY MEL SIMONS:

The Old-Time Radio Trivia Book

The Old-Time Television Trivia Book

Old-Time Radio Memories

The Show-Biz Trivia Book

Old-Time Television Memories

The Movie Trivia Book

Voices from the Philco

The Good Music Trivia Book

The Mel Simons Joke Book: If It's Laughter You're After

The Old-Time Radio Trivia Book II

The Old-Time Radio Trivia Book II

by Mel Simons

BearManor Media
2015

The Comedians Trivia Book

© 2015 Mel Simons

For information, address:

BearManor Media
P. O. Box 71426
Albany, GA 31708

bearmanormedia.com

Typesetting and layout by John Teehan

Published in the USA by BearManor Media

ISBN — 1-59393-767-9
978-1-59393-767-6

Dedication

I have been on WBZ radio in Boston for the past thirty-four years. This book is dedicated to the four talk-show hosts who I have been with:

Larry Glick – Bob Raleigh
Steve LeVeille – Morgan White, Jr.

I have loved working with the four of you.

Mel Simons
www.melsimons.net

The Four Aces and Mel Simons

(left to right) Harry Heisler, Fred Diodati, Mel, Joe Giglio,
Danny Colingo

The Four Aces

Foreword

I have been a nostalgia junkie for the past twenty years. I thought I knew everything there was to know until I read Mel Simons's *THE COMEDIANS TRIVIA BOOK*. It is informative, enlightening, and often quite surprising, in my opinion. There was no way Mel could write anything more enjoyable than his ten previous books. I was wrong. This is the grand-daddy of them all. I know you will love Mel's *THE COMEDIANS TRIVIA BOOK* as much as my partners and I have.

– *Fred Diodati*
Lead singer of The Four Aces

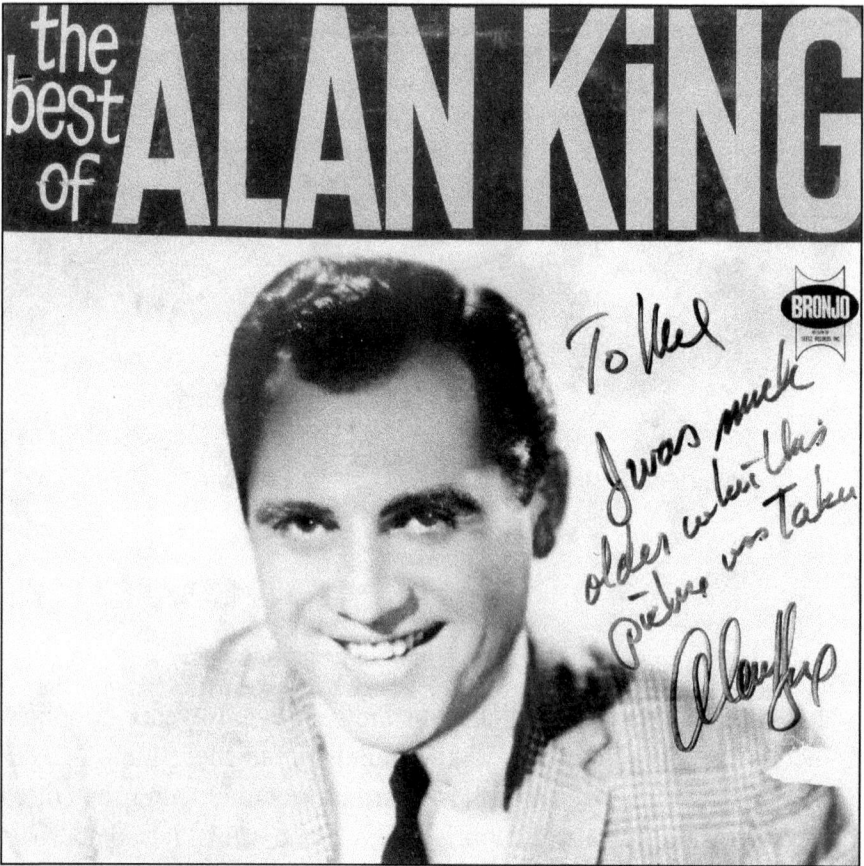

Alan King

Quiz #1

GENERAL KNOWLEDGE

(Answers on page 109)

1. Ted Knight played which character on *The Mary Tyler Moore Show?*

2. Who played José Jimenez?

3. Name the comedian/songwriter who was once a Harvard professor.

4. Which instrument did Morey Amsterdam play?

5. Who was the star of *Welcome Back, Kotter?*

6. Name Carol Burnett's two second bananas.

7. What is Bud Abbott's real first name?

8. How old did Jack Benny claim to be?

9. Who played Uncle Tonoose on *The Danny Thomas Show?*

10. Name the comedian who is the master of malapropism.

Art Carney

Quiz #2

MATCH THE COMEDIAN WITH HIS WIFE

(Answers on page 109)

1. Rob Petrie
2. Phil Harris
3. Chester A. Riley
4. Goodman Ace
5. Ed Norton
6. Peter Lind Hayes
7. Jim Anderson
8. Ernie Kovacs
9. Oliver Douglas
10. Eddie Cantor

    a. Trixie
    b. Laura
    c. Margaret
    d. Ida
    e. Edie
    f. Peg
    g. Alice
    h. Lisa
    i. Jane
    j. Mary

Bob Hope

Quiz #3

BOB HOPE
(Answers on Page 110)

1. What year was Bob Hope born?
2. In which country was he born?
3. What was his real name?
4. He used what name when he became a boxer?
5. Name his first Broadway show.
6. Name his first movie.
7. What song did he introduce, in which movie?
8. Name the singer who was his best friend?
9. How many "Road Movies" did he make?
10. What was his favorite sport?

W.C. Fields

Quiz #4

MATCH THE COMEDIAN WITH THE CATCH PHRASE

(Answers on Page 110)

1. Mary Tyler Moore
2. Dana Carvey
3. Tommy Smothers
4. Louis Nye
5. Bea Arthur
6. Rowan & Martin
7. Henny Youngman
8. Mae West
9. Phil Silvers
10. Art Carney

a. Isn't that special?
b. Take my wife, please!
c. Glad to see ya.
d. Oh, Rob . . .
e. Mom always liked you best.
f. GOD will get you for this.
g. Hi ho, Steverino.
h. Hey there, Ralphie boy.
i. You bet your bippy.
j. Why don't you come up and see me sometime?

Red Buttons

Quiz #5

TRUE OR FALSE
(Answers on Page 110)

1. Tom Poston was a regular on *The Steve Allen Show*.

2. Jackie Gleason's TV show was on Friday nights.

3. The song *My Mother's Eyes* was sung by George Jessel.

4. Rose Marie appeared in vaudeville as a dancer.

5. David Letterman has had a TV show on both NBC and CBS.

6. W. C. Fields was one of the stars of the Ziegfeld Follies.

7. Ralph Edwards hosted *People Are Talking*.

8. Pat Paulsen once ran for President of the United States.

9. The Smothers Brothers got their start on *The Tonight Show with Jack Paar*.

10. Jack Benny's announcer was Don Wilson.

Steve Allen

Quiz #6

GENERAL QUESTIONS
(Answers on Page 111)

1. What did Jackie Mason do before he became a comedian?

2. Who was the star of *That Girl?*

3. Which comedy team made the most appearances on *The Ed Sullivan Show?*

4. Who was the comic sidekick to Gene Autry?

5. Joan Davis was the star of which TV show?

6. What did Ed Norton do for a living?

7. Who played *My Little Margie?*

8. Name Alan Sherman's first album.

9. What is Jay Leno's hobby?

10. Who starred on radio's *My Friend Irma?*

DON ADAMS

PERSONAL MANAGEMENT
associates ltd.
beverly hills ·

Quiz #7

MATCH THE COMEDIAN WITH HIS CHARACTER

(Answers on Page 111)

1. Dana Carvey
2. Eddie Anderson
3. Tim Conway
4. Bob Denver
5. Buster Keaton
6. Bob Elliott
7. Mel Blanc
8. Phil Silvers
9. Freddie Prinze
10. Andy Kaufman

    a. Sergeant Bilko
    b. Dorf
    c. Wally Ballou
    d. The Church Lady
    e. Tony Clifton
    f. Pepe Le Pew
    g. Chico
    h. Rochester
    i. Gilligan
    j. The Great Stone Face

Dick Van Dyke

Quiz #8

DICK VAN DYKE
(Answers on Page 111)

1.   Who was Dick's comedy idol?

2.   Dick was married on which radio show?

3.   He won the Tony Award for which Broadway show?

4.   Dick costarred with Julie Andrews in which movie?

5.   Which character did he play in that movie?

6.   Name his best-known television show.

7.   What was his character's name on that show?

8.   Who played Buddy Sorrell on the show?

9.   Who created that TV show?

10.   Name Dick's brother, who is also a comedian?

Mel Simons and George Kirby

Quiz #9

MATCH THE COMEDIAN WITH THE CATCH PHRASE

(Answers on Page 112)

1. Lou Costello
2. Curly Howard
3. Jack Benny
4. Minnie Pearl
5. Pigmeat Markham
6. Bob Hope
7. Portland Hoffa
8. Frank Fontaine
9. Gertrude Berg
10. The Kingfish

    a. Yoo hoo, is anybody?
    b. Nyuk, nyuk, nyuk
    c. But I wanna tell ya
    d. Here come de judge
    e. Howdeeeee
    f. Holy mackerel, Andy!
    g. Well!
    h. Hi ya, Joe. Hi ya, Mr. Dunaheeeeeee.
    i. I'm a ba-a-a-d boy.
    j. Mr. Allen, Mr. Allen

Phil Silvers

Quiz #10

GENERAL QUESTIONS
(Answers on Page 112)

1. Rowan and Martin hosted which TV show?

2. Name the three Ritz Brothers.

3. Yakov Smirnoff is from what country?

4. Who was The Old Philosopher?

5. Gabe Kaplan has done a one-man show, playing which comedian?

6. Comedian Mark Russell played which instrument?

7. Name the duo that played The Bickersons.

8. Who hosted TV's *The Comedy Shop?*

9. Howard Morris was a second banana to which comedian?

10. Who played Ish Kabibble?

Myron Cohen and Mel Simons

Quiz #11

MATCH THE ACTOR WITH HIS MOVIE
(Answers on Page 112)

1. Chevy Chase
2. W. C. Fields
3. Eddie Murphy
4. Jack Benny
5. Rodney Dangerfield
6. Eddie Cantor
7. Danny DeVito
8. Mickey Rooney
9. Bert Lahr
10. Joe E. Brown

a. *The Wizard of Oz*
b. *Some Like It Hot*
c. *Back to School*
d. *The Bank Dick*
e. *Throw Mama From the Train*
f. *Three Amigos*
g. *The Absent-Minded Professor*
h. *Whoopie*
i. *The Horn Blows At Midnight*
j. *Love Finds Andy Hardy*

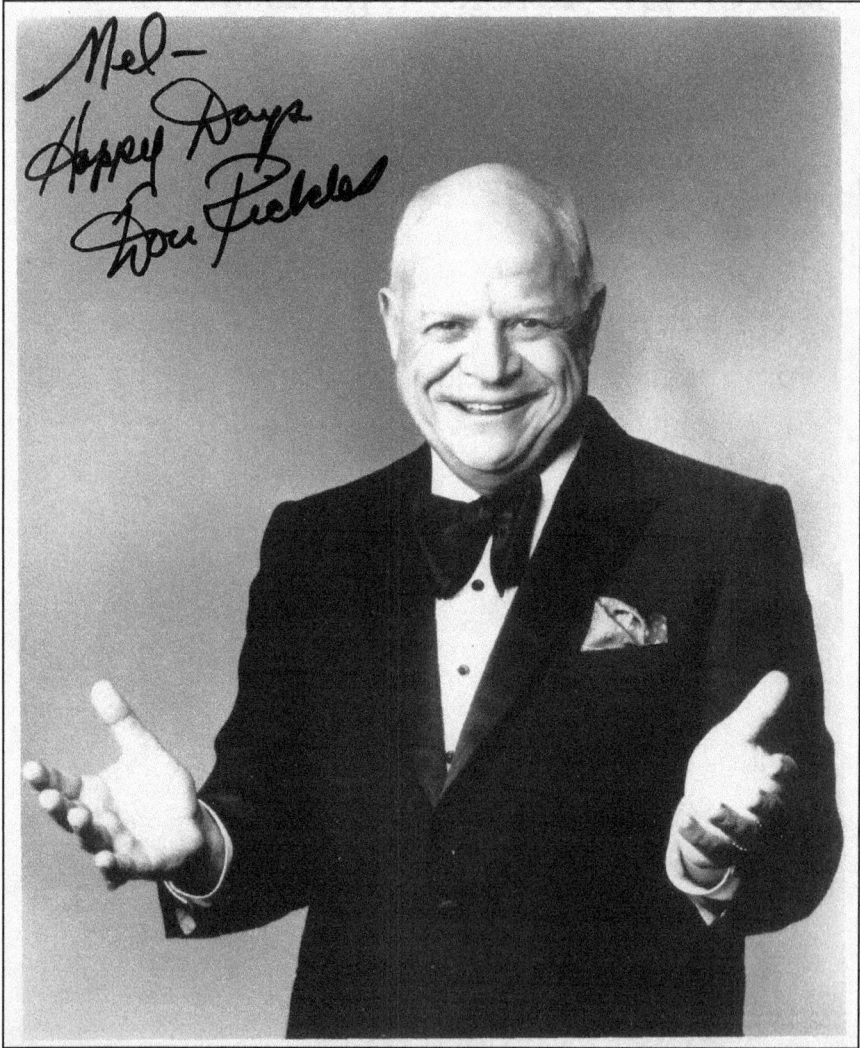

Don Rickles

Quiz #12

DON RICKLES

(Answers on Page 113)

1. What is Don's nickname?

2. Who gave him that nickname?

3. Don is the king of what type of comedy?

4. In his early career, which comedian was Don often compared to?

5. Who gave Don his start on television?

6. Don appeared over 100 times on which famous television show?

7. Name Don's best-selling record album.

8. Name the sitcom in which he starred.

9. What is Don's favorite phrase when he does standup?

10. Name the comedian who is his closest friend.

Carl Reiner

Quiz #13

MATCH THE COMMEDIENNE WITH HER CHARACTER
(Answers on Page 113)

1. Jean Stapleton
2. Marlo Thomas
3. Bea Arthur
4. Eve Arden
5. Valerie Harper
6. Lily Tomlin
7. Audrey Meadows
8. Minerva Pious
9. Vivian Vance
10. Fanny Brice

    a. "that girl"
    b. Ernestine
    c. Edith Bunker
    d. "our Miss Brooks"
    e. Rhoda
    f. Ethel Mertz
    g. Mrs. Nussbaum
    h. Maude
    i. Alice Kramden
    j. Baby Snooks

Quiz #14

MULTIPLE CHOICE
(Answers on Page 113)

1. Name the comedian who wrote the song "Nancy With the Laughing Face."
   a) Phil Foster   b) Phil Silvers c) Eddie Cantor

2. Whose real name is Karen Johnson?
   a) Nancy Walker   b) Linda Lavin   c) Whoopie Goldberg

3. Mr. Kitzel was a character on which radio show?
   a) Jack Benny   b) Eddie Cantor   c) Burns & Allen

4. Who was a regular on TV's *Laugh-In*?
   a) Lily Tomlin   b) Martha Raye   c) Goldie Hawn

5. Neil Simon wrote for which comedian?
   a) Milton Berle   b) Henry Morgan   c) Sid Caesar

6. Who was the comedian who often opened for Frank Sinatra?
   a) Pat Henry   b) Pat Cooper   c) Shecky Greene

7. The Nairobi Trio starred which comedian?
   a) Sid Caesar   b) Ernie Kovacs   c) Tim Conway

8. Which Eddie played Rochester?
   a) Eddie Murphy   b) Eddie Bracken   c) Eddie Anderson

9. Who played the accordion?
   a) Judy Tenuta   b) Larry Storch   c) Rita Rudner

10. The Little Rascals' dog was named
   a) Rover   b) Spot   c) Petey

Quiz #15

COMEDY TEAMS: Match the Partners
(Answers on Page 114)

1. Mike Nichols
2. Mel Brooks
3. Jack Burns
4. Sid Caesar
5. Ralph Kramden
6. Amos Jones
7. Jimmy Durante
8. Ole Olson
9. Bert Wheeler
10. Stump

a. Imogene Coca
b. Ed Norton
c. Chick Johnson
d. Andy Brown
e. Elaine May
f. Carl Reiner
g. Eddie Jackson
h. Stumpy
i. Avery Schreiber
j. Robert Woolsey

Victor Borge

Quiz #16

GENERAL QUESTIONS
(Answers on Page 114)

1. Who played Sheriff Andy Taylor?

2. What was Jimmy Walker's nickname on *Good Times?*

3. Name the comedian who had a long-time feud with Charlie McCarthy on radio.

4. Who was Jimmy Edmonson?

5. TV show, *You'll Never Get Rich*, starred which comedian?

6. *The Bickersons* got their start on which radio show?

7. Who was known as "A Wild and Crazy Guy?"

8. "Sock it to me" was a phrase that was used on which television show?

9. Who was known as "The Master of the Slow Burn?"

10. Ford Sterling was the leader of which silent movie comedy group?

Mel Simons and Milton Berle

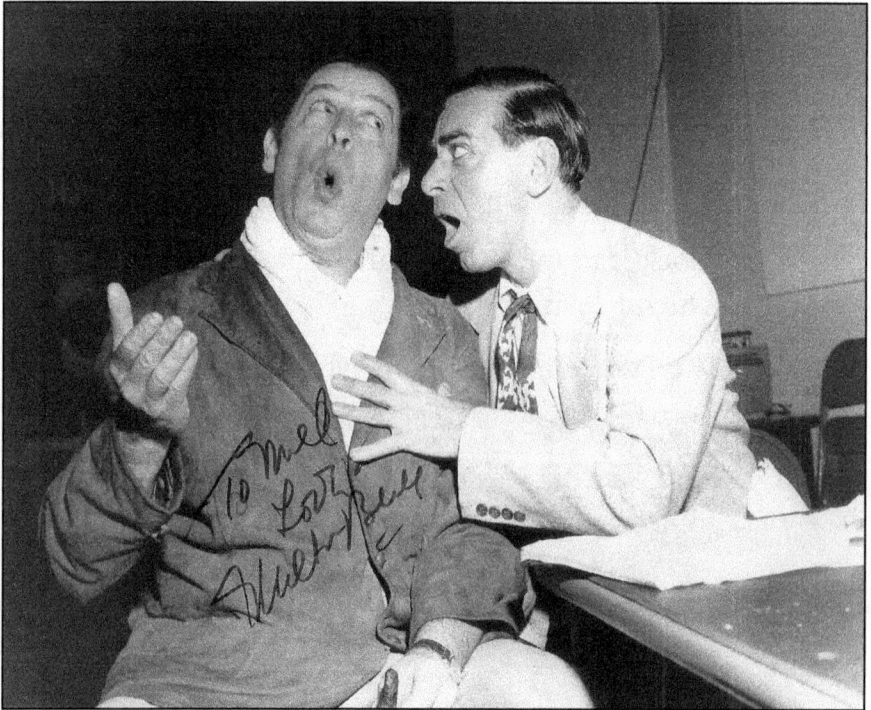

Milton Berle and Eddie Cantor

Quiz #17

MILTON BERLE
(Answers on Page 114)

1. What was Milton's nickname?

2. At the age of five he won a look-alike contest. Name the comedian he was imitating.

3. What was his mother's first name?

4. Milton got his start on radio on whose show?

5. Name the cigarette that sponsored *The Milton Berle Show* on radio.

6. What was the name of Milton's blockbuster TV show?

7. What was the name of his second TV show?

8. Both TV shows were on which night of the week?

9. On the first TV show, who did the commercials every week?

10. Who replaced that person doing commercials?

Quiz #18

MATCH THE COMEDIAN WITH HIS MOVIE
(Answers on Page 115)

1.   Adam Sandler

2.   Jack Lemmon

3.   Charlie Chaplin

4.   Woody Allen

5.   Jerry Lewis

6.   Danny Thomas

7.   Kevin James

8.   Red Skelton

9.   Steve Martin

10. Billy Crystal

a.   *Annie Hall*

b.   *Mr. Saturday Night*

c.   *The Jazz Singer*

d.   *The Bellboy*

e.   *Mr. Roberts*

f.   *The Mall Cop*

g.   *Modern Times*

h.   *The Jerk*

i.   *The Wedding Singer*

j.   *The Fuller Brush Man*

Quiz #19

GENERAL QUESTIONS
(Answers on Page 115)

1.   Name the clown on *The Howdy Doody Show.*

2.   What was the title of Martin and Lewis's first movie?

3.   Who was the voice of Daffy Duck?

4.   Who played Crazy Guggenheim on *Jackie Gleason: American Scene Magazine?*

5.   Doc Severinsen was the orchestra leader for which comedian?

6.   Name the comedian who starred in TV's *Monk and Mindy.*

7.   Name the comedian who hosted *Broadway Open House.*

8.   Wally Cox played which character on television?

9.   Who was known as the sneezing comedian?

10.   Name the radio comedian who invented the musical instrument the "bazooka."

Shelley Berman

Quiz #20

MATCH THE COMEDIAN WITH HIS CHARACTER

(Answers on Page 115)

1. Art Carney
2. Red Skelton
3. Paul Reubens
4. Phil Silvers
5. Al Lewis
6. Cliff Arquette
7. William Frawley
8. Robert Guillaume
9. Pat Harrington, Jr.
10. Wally Cox

   a. Grandpa Munster
   b. Sergeant Bilko
   c. Guido Panzini
   d. Charlie Weaver
   e. Ed Norton
   f. Mr. Peepers
   g. Pee-Wee Herman
   h. Benson
   i. Fred Mertz
   j. Clem Kadiddlehopper

Rodney Dangerfield

Quiz #21

OLD-TIME RADIO COMEDY SHOWS
(Answers on Page 116)

1. Who played Henry Aldrich?

2. What was Popeye's favorite food?

3. Johnson's Wax sponsored which husband-and-wife comedy team?

4. Who was known as "The Perfect Foil?"

5. On *The Burns & Allen Show*, who played "The Happy Postman?"

6. Name the star of the show *My Friend Irma*.

7. Who was known as "Banjo Eyes?"

8. What subject did Our Miss Brooks teach?

9. Amos and Andy belong to what lodge?

10. Who is Sadie Marks?

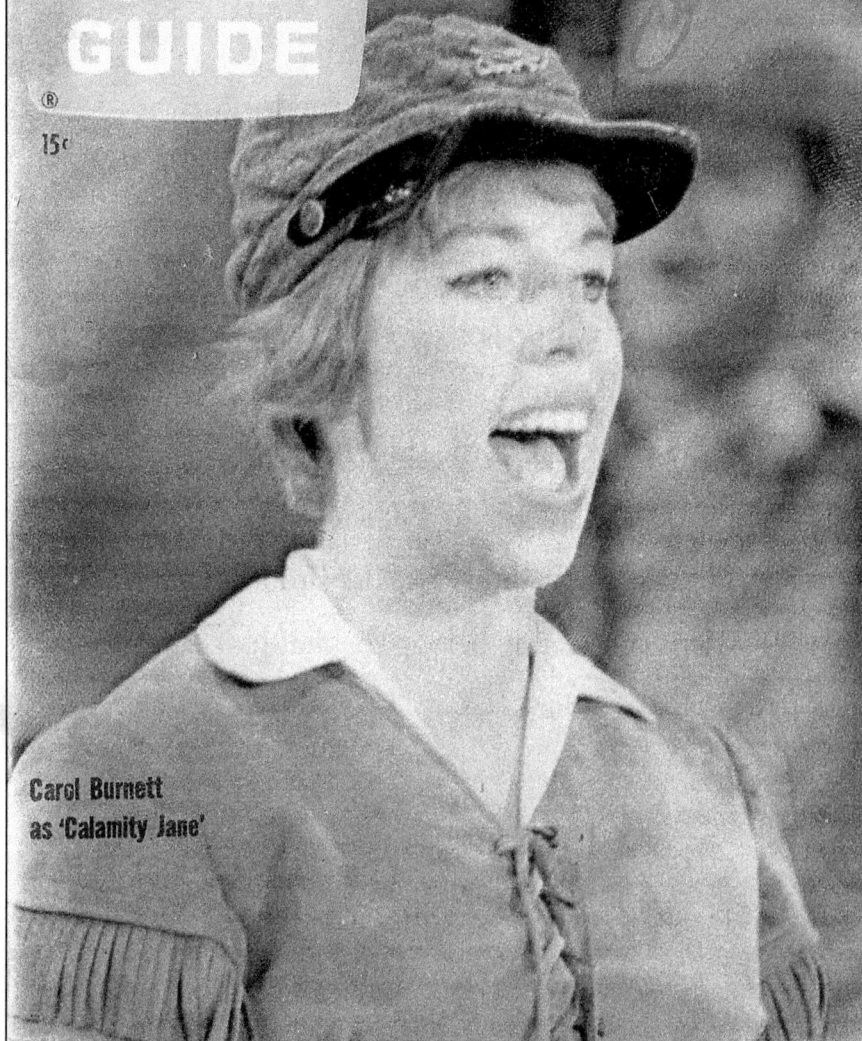

Carol Burnett

Quiz #22

CAROL BURNETT
(Answers on Page 116)

1.   Who raised Carol?

2.   Which lady did Carol idolize?

3.   Name the first novelty song that Carol sang.

4.   Carol won a Tony Award for which Broadway show?

5.   She became a regular in 1956 on whose TV show?

6.   *The Carol Burnett Show* was the last popular variety show on television. How many years was it on?

7.   Which college did Carol attend?

8.   When Carol did her famous yell, who was she imitating?

9.   At the end of her show, Carol would always touch her left ear. What did this signify?

10. Carol performed in a two-woman show at Carnegie Hall. Who was her costar?

Mel Simons and Dick Shawn

Quiz #23

COMMEDIENES QUIZ
(Answers on Page 116)

1. Who played Laverne and Shirley?

2. Name the lady who always said "Can we talk?"

3. Whose real name is Sophie Feldman?

4. What character did Betty White play on *The Golden Girls?*

5. Name the two television shows that starred Gale Storm.

6. Rita Rudner has her own club in which city?

7. Who was known as the first lady of stand-up?

8. Name the comedienne who had a hit record "Abraham, Martin, and John?"

9. Who was the female star of *The Ziegfeld Follies* for many years?

10. What musical instrument did Kaye Ballard play?

Jonathan Winters

Quiz #24

MATCH THE COMEDIAN WITH THE CORRECT RECORD ALBUM

(Answers on Page 117)

1. "My Son, the Folk Singer"
2. "The 2,000 Year Old Man"
3. "Comedy in Music"
4. "The Buttoned-Down Mind"
5. "The World According to Me"
6. "Child of the 50's"
7. "Madcap Musical Nonsense At Your House"
8. "The First Family"
9. "Class Clown"
10. "Everybody Gotta Be Someplace"

  a. The Three Stooges
  b. Bob Newhart
  c. Jackie Mason
  d. Robert Klein
  e. Alan Sherman
  f. George Carlin
  g. Mel Brooks and Carl Reiner
  h. Victor Borge
  i. Vaughn Meader
  j. Myron Cohen

Flip Wilson

Quiz #25

RADIO AND TELEVISION COMEDIANS

From the following list of comedians: five appeared on radio, five appeared on television, five appeared on both. Who appeared on what?

(Answers on Page 117)

Milton Berle

Goodman Ace

Redd Foxx

Don Adams

Ed Wynn

Fred Allen

Fanny Brice

Dick Van Dyke

Phil Harris – Alice Faye

George Burns

Jack Pearl

Gertrude Berg

Bob Newhart

Carol Burnett

Joe Penner

Pat Cooper

Quiz #26

GENERAL QUESTIONS
(Answers on Page 118)

1. Name the comedian/cowboy that discovered Gene Autry.

2. The song "Near You" was the theme song of which comedian?

3. What type of character did Foster Brooks play?

4. Who was Ed Norton married to?

5. Name the comedian who was featured in the movie *Back to School*.

6. What was the name of Billy Crystal's Broadway show?

7. Name the comedian who said "…never got a dinner?"

8. Who was known as "The Little Tramp?"

9. How many years was Red Skelton on television?

10. What was Whoopi Goldberg's first movie?

Shecky Greene

Shecky Greene

Thanks mel
Pick a
mood.

Quiz #27

COMEDY TEAMS: Match the partners
(Answers on Page 118)

1. Dean Martin
2. Bud Abbott
3. George Burns
4. Mike Nichols
5. Lum
6. Marty Allen
7. Stan Laurel
8. Johnny Wayne
9. Penn
10. Ole Olsen

   a. Oliver Hardy
   b. Elaine May
   c. Abner
   d. Jerry Lewis
   e. Gracie Allen
   f. Teller
   g. Steve Rossi
   h. Lou Costello
   i. Frank Shuster
   j. Chick Johnson

Mel Simons and Henny Youngman

Quiz #28

MOREY AMSTERDAM and HENNY YOUNGMAN
Is it Morey or Henny?

(Answers on Page 118)

1.   Who got their start on Kate Smith's radio show?

2.   Who was born in England?

3.   Milton Berle helped which one get his start in comedy?

4.   What instrument did Henny play?

5.   Who was known as the "human joke machine?"

6.   When Al Capone needed a laugh, who did he often send for?

7.   Whose wife was named Sadie?

8.   Who began his career as a printer?

9.   Who got his big break appearing on *The Kate Smith* [radio] *Show?*

10.   Who played Buddy Sorrell on television?

11.   Who wrote the song "Rum and Coca-Cola?"

Morey Amsterdam

Quiz #29

MATCH THE COMEDIAN WITH THEIR CATCH PHRASE

(Answers on Page 119)

1. Jackie Gleason
2. Joan Rivers
3. Jim Nabors
4. Rodney Dangerfield
5. Joe Penner
6. Jack Benny
7. Bob and Ray
8. Carol Burnett
9. Don Rickles
10. Jack Paar

    a. Can we talk?
    b. Hello, dummy.
    c. Now cut that out!
    d. Hardy har-har.
    e. Write if you get work.
    f. Golly!
    g. Wanna buy a duck?
    h. No respect.
    i. I kid you not.
    j. I'm so glad we had this time together.

Bob Newhart

Quiz #30

MULTIPLE CHOICE
(Answers on Page 119)

1. Who was known as the "Ultimate Vegas Comedian?"
a) Louis Prima   b) Shecky Greene   c) Jack E. Leonard

2. Bill Cosby played which cartoon character?
a) Wimpy   b) Bart Simpson   c) Fat Albert

3. Where was Howie Mandel born?
a) New York City   b) Toronto   c) Las Vegas

4. Name the comedian on *The Steve Allen Show* that would always forget?
a) Tom Poston   b) Louis Nye   c) Bill Dana

5. Who was known as "The Thief of Bad Gags?"
a) Milton Berle   b) Bob Hope   c) Jerry Colonna

6. Who did President Harry Truman name as the "Toastmaster General of the United States?"
a) Groucho Marx   b) Harry Ritz   c) George Jessel

7. Name the comedian who once used the name Jack Roy.
a) Lenny Bruce   b) Rodney Dangerfield   c) Mort Sahl

8. What silent screen comedian was known for hanging on a high clock?
a) Harold Lloyd   b) Ben Turpin   c) Fatty Arbuckle

9. Name the comedian who wrote the song "Smile."
a) Jerry Colonna   b) Charlie Chaplin   c) Buck Henry

10 Who was known as "Lonesome George?"
a) George Burns   b) George Kirby   c) George Gobel

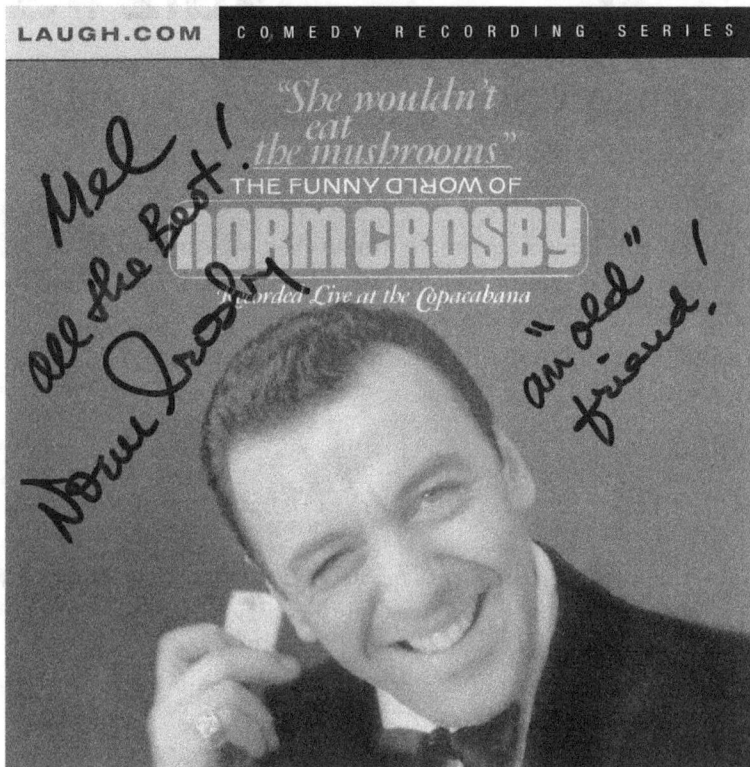

Norm Crosby

Mel Simons and Norm Crosby

Quiz #31

MATCH THE COMEDIAN WITH HIS CHARACTER
(Answers on Page 119)

1. Alan Alda
2. Don Adams
3. Jackie Gleason
4. Flip Wilson
5. Jim Backus
6. Redd Foxx
7. Fred Gwynn
8. Johnny Carson
9. Mel Blanc
10. Tony Randall

a. Flex Unger
b. Art Fern
c. Bugs Bunny
d. Geraldine
e. The Poor Soul
f. Herman Munster
g. Sanford
h. Hawkeye
i. Mr. Magoo
i. Maxwell Smart

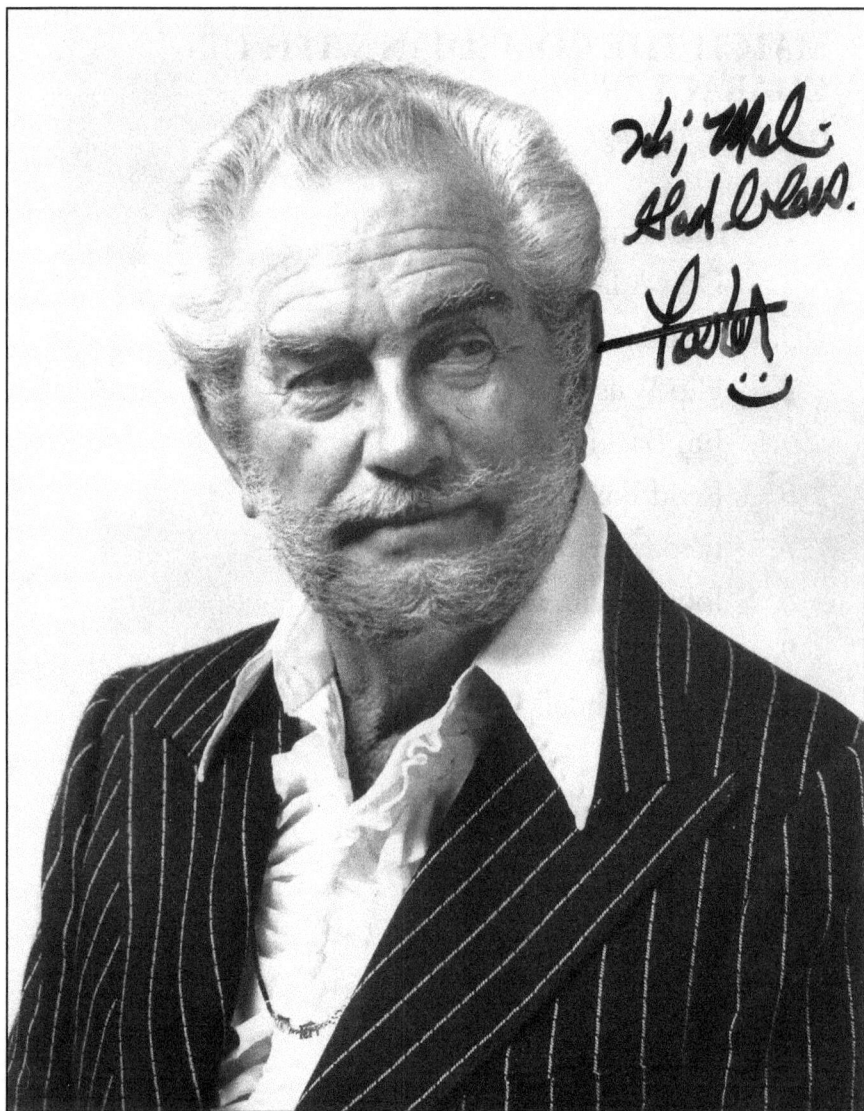

Foster Brooks

Quiz #32

GENERAL QUESTIONS
(Answers on Page 120)

1. Name the silent screen comedian who was cross-eyed.

2. Radio and TV's *The Life of Riley* featured which comedian?

3. Who was the most popular comedy team of the 1950s?

4. Who played Barney Fife?

5. Portland Hoffa was married to what well-known radio comedian?

6. *The Jeffersons* was a spin-off of what television show?

7. Who played Gomer Pyle?

8. Name Jack Benny's vocal group.

9. Who was the first Alice on *The Honeymooners?*

10. Henry Morgan was a panelist on what TV show?

Abbott and Costello

Quiz #33

MARCH THE COMEDIAN WITH HIS MOVIE
(Answers on Page 120)

1. Dick Van Dyke
2. Rodney Dangerfield
3. George Burns
4. Jackie Gleason
5. John Belushi
6. Eddie Murphy
7. Zero Mostel
8. Leslie Nielsen
9. Danny Kaye
10. Bert Lahr

   a. *Oh, God!*
   b. *Mary Poppins*
   c. *Naked Gun*
   d. *Beverly Hills Cop*
   e. *The Producers*
   f. *Caddyshack*
   g. *The Blues Brothers*
   h. *The Inspector General*
   i. *The Hustler*
   j. *The Wizard of Oz*

Quiz #34

COMEDIENNES
(Answers on Page 120)

1. Who was married to Fang?

2. Eve Arden starred in what radio and TV show?

3. Who played Edith Ann?

4. Who won the Academy Award for *Cactus Flower?*

5. Name the gal known as "The Goddess."

6. Who is Caryn Johnson?

7. Gertrude Berg created what show?

8. Who played Maude?

9. Lulu McConnell appeared on what radio show?

10. Darla Hood appeared in what movie shorts?

Quiz #35

MATCH THE COMEDIAN WITH HIS CATCHPHRASE

(Answers on Page 121)

1. Billy Crystal
2. Flip Wilson
3. Oliver Hardy
4. Jimmy Walker
5. Ted Knight
6. Jackie Vernon
7. Joe Penner
8. Yakov Smirnoff
9. Jim Nabors
10. Joe E. Lewis

a. Hi, guys.
b. The devil made me do it.
c. You look marvelous.
d. What a country!
e. Dyn-o-mite!
f. Shazam!
g. Hello again, fun seekers.
h. You nasty man!
i. Here's another fine mess you've gotten me into.
j. It is now post time.

Steven Wright

Quiz #36

TRUE OR FALSE
(Answers on Page 121)

1. Redd Foxx began his career as a singer.

2. Buddy Hackett had a hit single called "The Chinese Waiter."

3. Minnie was the mother of The Ritz Brothers.

4. Jack Benny, on radio, was sponsored by Old Gold.

5. The show *The Producers* was written by Mel Brooks.

6. Baba Wawa was played by Joan Rivers.

7. The movie *The Joker is Wild* was the life story of Joe E. Brown.

8. Karnak The Magnificent was Johnny Carson.

9. Sid Caesar was once a musician, playing the trumpet.

10. "Dr. Kronkheit and His Only Living Patient" was done by Abbott and Costello.

Joey Bishop

Quiz #37

GENERAL QUESTIONS
(Answers on Page 121)

1. Who is Pasquale Caputo?

2. Which comedian made the most HBO specials?

3. Sam Levenson taught what subject in high school?

4. Who was the first host of *The Tonight Show?*

5. Who played Amos 'n' Andy on the radio?

6. Which comedian was known as "The Great Stone Face?"

7. Bob Newhart has a degree in what?

8. Jack Benny had a famous car. What was it?

9. Name Willie Howard's brother.

10. Who starred in TV's *I Married Joan?*

Jackie Gleason

Quiz #38

JACKIE GLEASON
(Answers on Page 122)

1. What was Jackie's nickname?

2. When Jackie left high school, what did he do for a living?

3. What was his first television show?

4. Name his first TV variety show.

5. What night of the week was *The Jackie Gleason Show* on?

6. Name the character who Art Carney played on *The Honeymooners*.

7. Name the three ladies who played Alice Kramden.

8. What did Ralph Kramden do for work?

9. Name the character played by Frank Fortaine.

10. Gleason won the Tony Award for what Broadway show?

Quiz #39

MATCH THE COMEDIAN WITH HIS WIFE
(Answers on Page 122)

1.   Mel Brooks
2.   Steve Allen
3.   Ralph Kramden
4.   Kingfish
5.   Bob Hope
6.   Danny DeVito
7.   Fred Mertz
8.   Danny Kaye
9.   Carl Reiner
10. Buddy Surrell

    a. Pickles
    b. Sylvia
    c. Ria
    d. Sapphire
    e. Jayne
    f. Ann
    g. Estelle
    h. Ethel
    i. Alice
    j. Delores

Quiz #40

OLD-TIME RADIO COMEDY SHOWS
(Answers on Page 122)

1. Pepsodent sponsored which comedian?

2. Aunt Fanny appeared on which radio show?

3. What was Baby Snooks's last name?

4. Who was Garry Moore's partner on radio?

5. Where did Lum and Abner work?

6. What were the first names of The Bickersons?

7. Tony Randall appeared on what radio show?

8. Pedro appeared as a character on what show?

9. Name the cigarette that sponsored Abbott and Costello on radio.

10. Victor Borge got his start on whose radio show?

Bill Dana

Quiz #41

MULTIPLE CHOICE
(Answers on Page 123)

1. Which Jack was born on Valentine's Day
a) Jack Paar   b) Jack Benny   c) Jack Oakie

2. Who was known as the crying comedian?
a) Orson Bean   c) Don Adams   c) Rip Taylor

3. Ed Sullivan had a feud with which comedian?
a) Jackie Mason   b) Woody Allen   c) Benny Hill

4. Who was married to Fang?
a) Totie Fields   b) Phyllis Diller   c) Eve Arden

5. Name the comedian who was an Academy Award winner.
a) Art Carney   b) Bob Hope   c) Gabe Kaplan

6. What lady was not on TV's *The Golden Girls?*
a) Bea Arthur   b) Betty White   c) Minnie Pearl

7. Who was offered the role of Archie Bunker?
a) Mickey Rooney   b) Jackie Cooper   c) Jerry Lester

8. Name the comedian who makes a living as a gambler.
a) Sherman Hemsley   b) Richard Lewis   c) Gabe Kaplan

9. Which comedian hosted the Academy Awards?
a) Johnny Carson   b) Alan King   c) David Letterman

10. Who was the master of double talk?
a) Al Kelly   b) Joey Adams   c) Lou Kelly

George Burns and Gracie Allen

Quiz #42

GEORGE BURNS AND GRACIE ALLEN
(Answers on Page 123)

1. What was George Burns's real name?

2. What was Gracie Allen's real name?

3. Name the vocal group that George organized when he was seven years old.

4. What did Gracie originally do in Vaudeville?

5. How many years were George and Gracie married?

6. What coffee company sponsored them on radio?

7. What role did Mel Blanc play on the radio show?

8. Who was their long-time sponsor on television?

9. George won the Academy Award as best supporting actor for what movie?

10. Who was originally scheduled to play that role?

Quiz #43

MATCH THE COMEDIAN WITH HIS CHARACTER

(Answers on Page 123)

1. Peter Sellers
2. Dana Carvey
3. Don Knotts
4. Larry Storch
5. Jack Klugman
6. Tim Moore
7. Harry Morgan
8. Joe E. Ross
9. Sherman Hemsley
10. William Bendix

a. Barney Fife
b. George Jefferson
c. Chester A. Riley
d. Oscar Madison
e. The Church Lady
f. Inspector Clouseau
g. The Kingfish
h. Gunther Toody
i. Corporal Agarn
j. Colonel Potter

Quiz #44

GENERAL QUESTIONS
(Answers on Page 124)

1. Eddie Murphy became a star on what television show?

2. Where was Victor Borge born?

3. Who never met a man he didn't like?

4. Woody Allen plays what musical instrument?

5. *The Little Rascals* were also known by what other name?

6. Robin Williams played which comic book character in a motion picture?

7. Who said "Hi-ho, Steverino?"

8. What is Buddy Hackett's real first name?

9. Name the comedian who hosted TV's *Treasure Hunt*.

10. Who were Marion and Jim Jordan?

Mel Simons and Jack Carter

Quiz #45

MATCH THE COMEDIAN WITH HIS WIFE
(Answers on Page 124)

1. Regis Philbin
2. Ozzie Nelson
3. Jerry Stiller
4. Ed Norton
5. Jerry Halper
6. Archie Bunker
7. Fred Allen
8. George Jefferson
9. Jack Benny
10. Gene Wilder

    a. Edith
    b. Louise
    c. Mary
    d. Gilda
    e. Joy
    f. Millie
    g. Harriet
    h. Trixie
    i. Portland
    j. Anne

Quiz #46

GENERAL QUESTIONS
(Answers on Page 124)

1. Allan Sherman created what television show?

2. Name the telephone operator that Lily Tomlin played on *Laugh-In*.

3. Who starred in TV's *The Odd Couple?*

4. *The Nairobi Trio* featured which comedian?

5. What are the first names of the Smothers Brothers?

6. Name the comedian who always says, "Why not?"

7. On the show *Seinfeld*, what was Kramer's first name?

8. Wally Cox starred in what television show?

9. Who is Bob Elliott's well-known son?

10. Paul Shaffer is the bandleader for which comedian?

Quiz #47

MATCH THE COMEDIAN WITH HIS MOVIE

(Answers on Page 125)

1. Robin Williams
2. Art Carney
3. Bob Hope
4. Richard Pryor
5. Walter Matthau
6. Billy Crystal
7. Buster Keaton
8. Mel Brooks
9. Groucho Marx
10. William Bendix

   a. *High Anxiety*
   b. *The Seven Little Foys*
   c. *The Sunshine Boys*
   d. *Harlem Nights*
   e. *When Harry Met Sally*
   f. *The Babe Ruth Story*
   g. *The General*
   h. *Animal Crackers*
   i. *Harry and Tonto*
   j. *Good Morning, Vietnam*

Bill Cosby

Quiz #48

BILL COSBY
(Answers on Page 125)

1. What city did Bill grow up in?

2. Name the college that he attended.

3. He got a scholarship to that college for what sport?

4. What did he do for a living before he became a comedian?

5. Who gave him his first break on television?

6. Bill costarred with Robert Culp in what TV adventure show?

7. He created what cartoon character?

8. Name the program that was his greatest success on television.

9. What was the name of the character he played on the show?

10. How many Grammy Awards has Bill won?

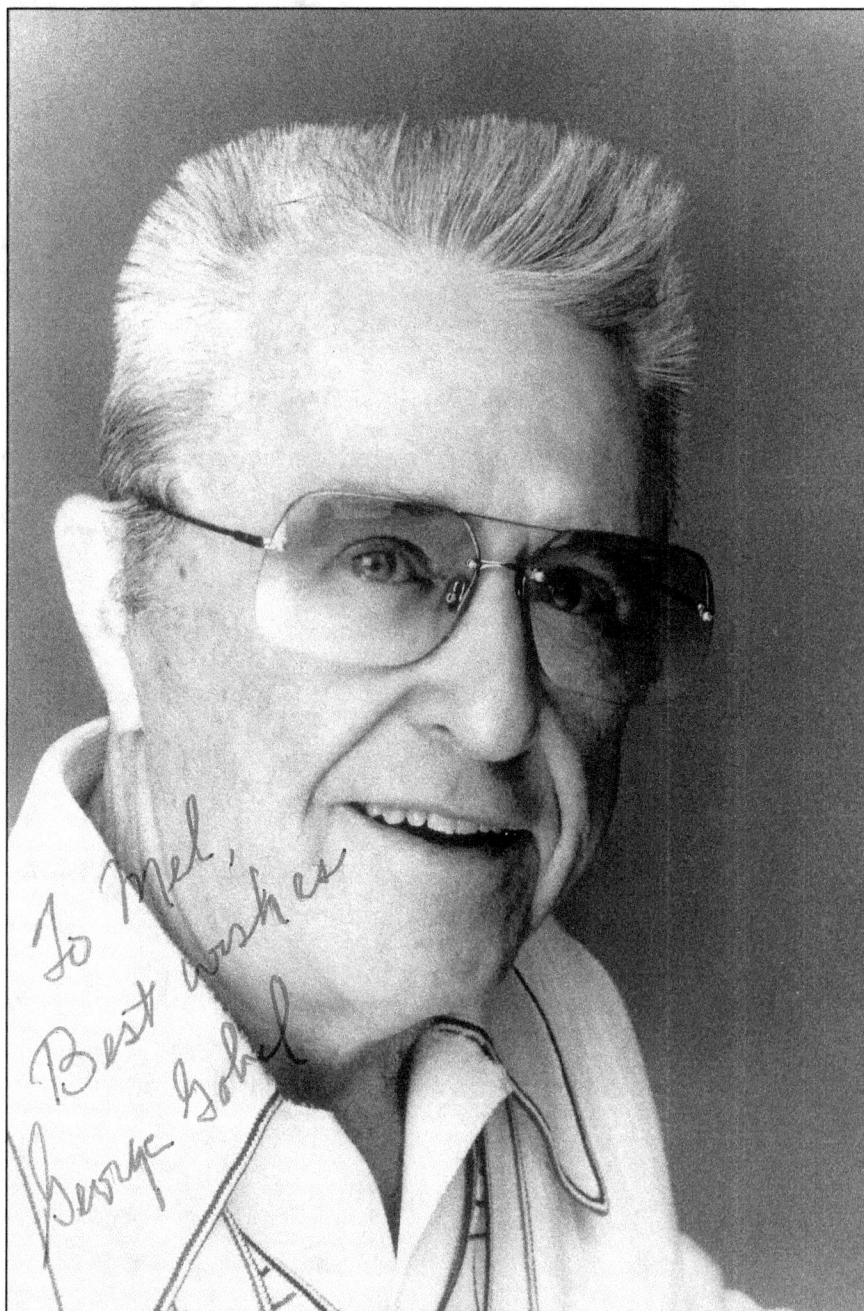

George Gobel

Quiz #49

MATCH THE COMEDIAN WITH THE CATCHPHRASE

(Answers on Page 125)

1. Billy Crystal
2. Jimmy Durante
3. Steve Martin
4. Don Adams
5. Leslie Nielsen
6. W. C. Fields
7. Fred Allen
8. Artie Johnson
9. Milton Berle
10. Red Buttons

a. Sorry about that, chief.
b. Never got a dinner.
c. Well, Portland, gee whiz.
d. Verrry interesting.
e. And don't call me Shirley.
f. Goodnight, Mrs. Calabash, wherever you are.
g. Well, excuuuuse me.
h. I swear I'll kill you.
i. Don't get me started.
j. Never give a sucker an even break.

Jerry Lewis

Quiz #50

GENERAL QUESTIONS
(Answers on Page 126)

1.   Who did Jimmy Durante say goodnight to?

2.   What night of the week was the Ken Murray TV show on?

3.   Who was Goodman Ace married to?

4.   Jack Benny had a feud with what famous radio comedian?

5.   Who was the crying comedian?

6.   Jerry Colonna was a second banana to whom?

7.   What do Harold Peary and Willard Waterman have in common?

8.   Who was the master of the slow burn?

9.   Name the comedian with the most appearances on *The Ed Sullivan Show?*

10.   Where did Vic and Sade live?

Bob & Ray

Quiz #51

COMEDY TEAMS: *Match the partner*
(Answers on Page 126)

1. Dan Rowan
2. Jerry Stiller
3. Homer
4. Fibber McGee
5. Cheech
6. Gallagher
7. Joe Smith
8. Jack Burns
9. Bob Elliot
10. Joe Weber

   a. Ray Goulding
   b. Chong
   c. Avery Schreiber
   d. Jethro
   e. Anne Meara
   f. Molly
   g. Dick Martin
   h. Shean
   i. Lew Fields
   j. Charlie Dale

Sid Caesar

Sid Caesar and Mel Simons

Quiz #52

SID CAESAR

(Answers on Page 126)

1. Name the famous music school that Sid attended.

2. What musical instrument did he play?

3. What was Sid's first television show?

4. Name his most famous television show.

5. Who created that show?

6. What night of the week was the show on?

7. Who was his costar?

8. Name the television show that was the spin-off.

9. Who was his costar on that show?

10. Who played his wife in the movie *It's a Mad, Mad, Mad, Mad World?*

Quiz #53

TRUE OR FALSE
(Answers on Page 127)

1. Red Skelton's first name was Richard.

2. Phil Harris once had a number-one record called "The Thing."

3. Abbott & Costello's most famous routine was "Slowly We Turn."

4. Comic Leonard Barr was Dean Martin's uncle.

5. Gladys Ormphby was plated by Judy Carne.

6. Rip Taylor threw confetti at the audience.

7. Sylvia Fine wrote comedy material for Danny Thomas.

8. One of The Little Rascals was Mickey Rooney.

9. Sam Cowling was a comedian on radio's *The Breakfast Club*.

10. Rodney Dangerfield once used the name Jack Roy.

Quiz #54

GENERAL QUESTIONS
(Answers on Page 127)

1. Who starred in the movie *Mrs. Doubtfire?*

2. What was Alan Sherman's biggest-selling 45?

3. Who hosted the most Academy Awards?

4. Eddie Lawrence played which character?

5. Name Abbott & Costello's most famous routine.

6. Who played the German spy on *Laugh-In?*

7. Marty Allen had two partners. Name them.

8. Name the TV character who used to say "Shazam!" and "Golly!"

9. Who was the most popular occupant of the center square on *The Hollywood Squares?*

10. Who was the first comedian to be honored by a U.S. Postage Stamp?

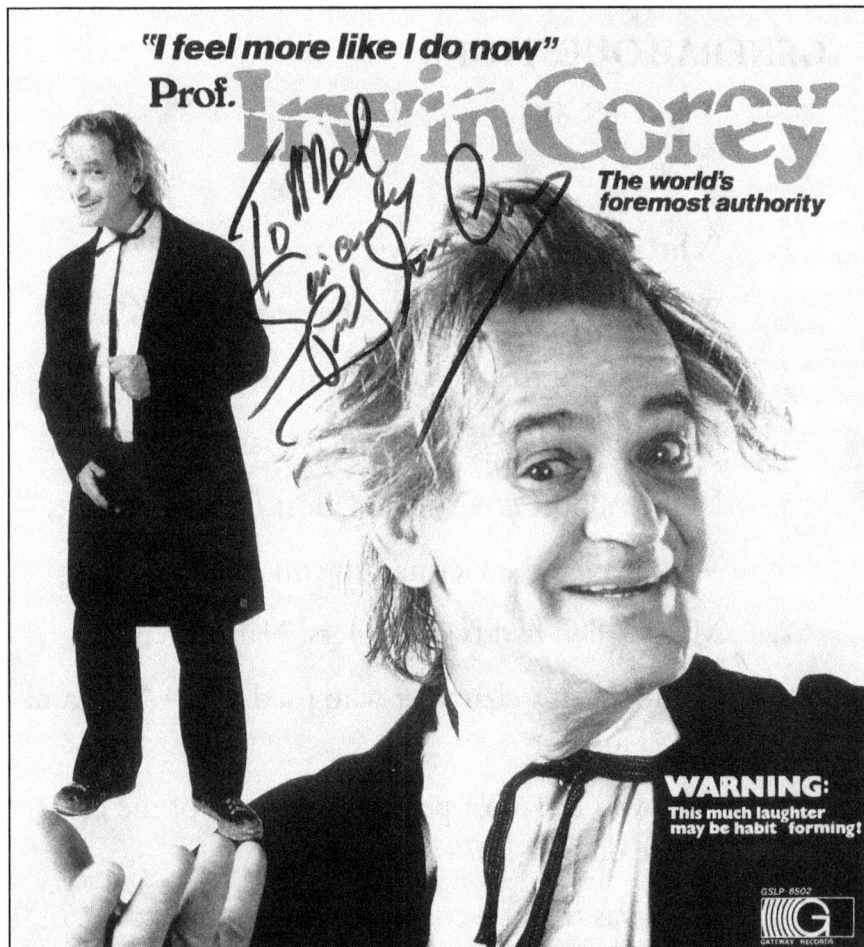

Professor Irwin Corey

Quiz #55

DANNY THOMAS
(Answers on Page 127)

1. What is Danny's real name?

2. Danny was a regular on what radio show?

3. He played the son of a Cantor in what movie?

4. Name his famous daughter.

5. She is married to whom?

6. Name Danny's famous television show.

7. How many years was the show on television?

8. What was his son's name on the TV show?

9. What character did Hans Conreid play on the show?

10. Danny founded what hospital?

Pat Henry and Mel Simons

Quiz #56

MULTIPLE CHOICE
(Answers on Page 128)

1. Valerie Harper starred in what TV sitcom?
a) *That Girl*   b)   *Rhoda*   c)   *Cybill*

2. Who sang "The Chanukah Song" on *Saturday Night Live?*
a) Eddie Murphy   b) Adam Sandler   c) Dana Carvey

3. Jack Benny had a fun feud with which comedian?
a) Eddie Cantor   b)   Groucho Marx   c)   Fred Allen

4. Who was once Redd Foxx's partner?
a) Slappy White   b)   Flip Wilson   c)   George Kirby

5. Name the comedian who wrote the book *I Owe Russia $1200?*
a) Yakov Smirnoff   b)   Dennis Miller   c)   Bob Hope

6. Nat Hiken wrote what popular TV show?
a) *The Phil Silvers Show* b)   *The Dick Van Dyke Show*
c) *I Love Lucy*

7. Who was Gene Autry's comic sidekick?
a) Jingles   b)   Gabby Hayes   c)   Pat Buttram

8. Who is the producer of *Saturday Night Live?*
a) Bill Paley   b)   Lorne Michaels   c)   Phil Foster

9. What musical instrument did Chico Marx play?
a) Piano   b)   Harp   c)   Drums

10. Who was Henry Morgan's radio sidekick?
a) Jackie Kelk   b)   Arnold Stang   c)   Pat Cooper

Rose Marie

Quiz #57

GENERAL QUESTIONS
(Answers on Page 128)

1. 1. Who played the Cowardly Lion in *The Wizard of Oz?*

2. Leo Gorcey was the head of what group?

3. The record album *The First Family* was created by whom?

4. Who created the character Maude Frickert?

5. How many years did Jay Leno host *The Tonight Show?*

6. Abe Vigoda played which character on *Barney Miller?*

7. Who created and wrote *The Dick Van Dyke Show?*

8. Fanny Brice played which character on radio?

9. Name Ozzie and Harriet's two sons.

10. Who did stand-up comedy reading from the newspaper?

Lucille Ball

Quiz #58

LUCILLE BALL
(Answers on Page 128)

1. What color was Lucy's hair?

2. Name her popular radio show.

3. Who was her costar on that show?

4. What years was *I Love Lucy* on television?

5. Name her TV show that was on from 1962-1968.

6. Name her TV show that was on from 1968-1974.

7. Name Lucy's famous husband.

8. What was her name on *I Love Lucy?*

9. Name Lucy's Broadway show.

10. Name the movie Lucy appeared in that came from a Broadway show.

Mel Simons and George Jessel

Quiz #59

MATCH THE COMEDIAN WITH THE CATCHPHRASE
(Answers on Page 129)

1. Don Adams
2. George Gobel
3. Marty Allen
4. George Jessel
5. Steve Martin
6. Peter Falk
7. Joe Besser
8. Freddie Prinze
9. The Mad Russian
10. Jackie Gleason

    a. It's not my job.
    b. Not so hard.
    c. How do you do?
    d. And away we go.
    e. Missed me by that much.
    f. I'm a wild and crazy guy.
    g. Am I bothering you?
    h. Hello, Mama?
    i. Well, I'll be a dirty bird.
    j. Hello dere.

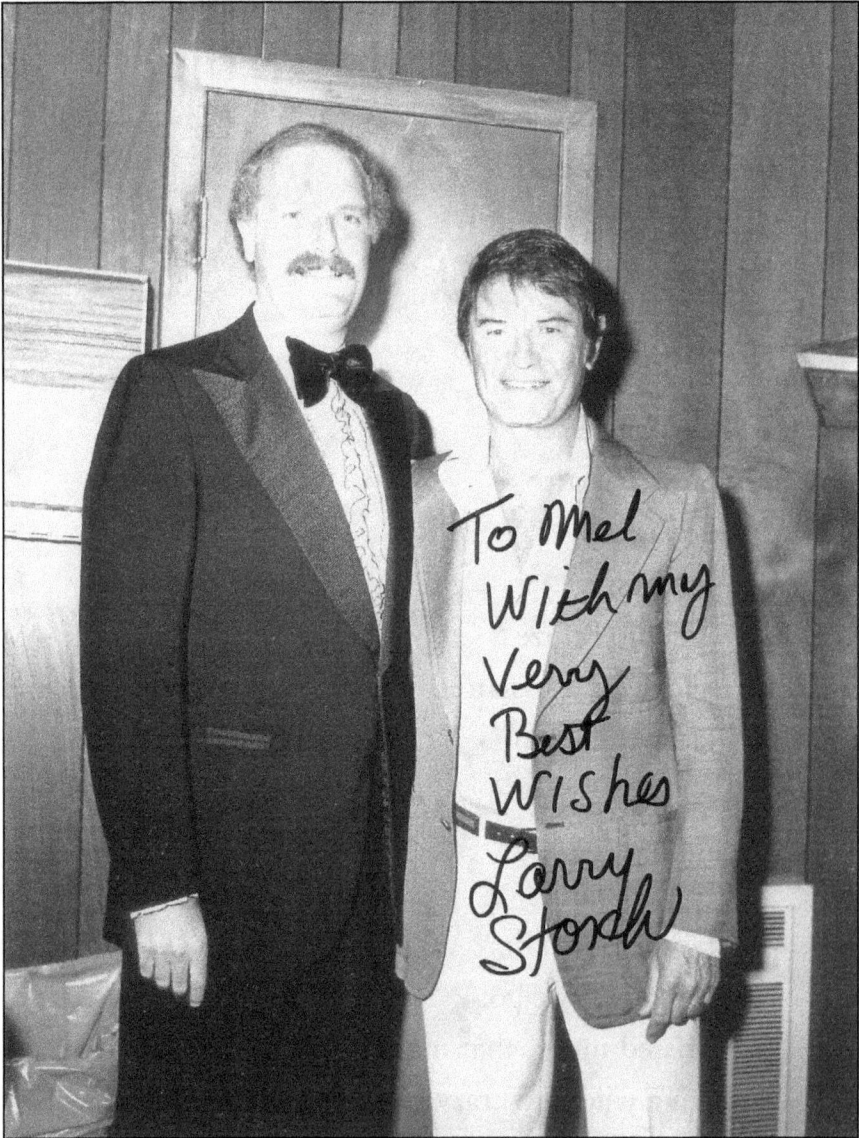

Mel Simons and Larry Storch

Quiz #60

GENERAL QUESTIONS
(Answers on Page 129)

1. Gilda Radner was married to which comedian?

2. Who was the 2,000-year-old man?

3. The movie *The Sunshine Boys* was based on which comedy team?

4. Name the comedian known as "The Professor."

5. Who played Betty Boop?

6. What did Archie Bunker often call his son-in-law?

7. Who played Aunt Blabby?

8. Name the lady known as "The Last of the Red Hot Mamas."

9. Who is Joe Yule, Jr.?

10. What was the name of Buddy Hackett's hit record?

Jackie Mason and Mel Simons

ANSWERS

QUIZ #1 *(from page 3)*

1. Ted Baxter
2. Bill Dana
3. Tom Lehrer
4. The cello
5. Gabe Kaplan
6. Tim Conway and Harvey Korman
7. William
8. Thirty-nine
9. Hans Conreid
10. Norm Crosby

QUIZ #2 *(from page 5)*

1. b
2. g
3. f
4. i
5. a
6. j
7. c
8. e
9. h
10. d

QUIZ #3 *(from page 7)*

1. 1903
2. England
3. Leslie Townes Hope
4. Packy East
5. Red, Hot and Blue
6. The Big Broadcast of 1938
7. "Thanks For the Memory"
8. Bing Crosby
9. Seven
10. Golf

QUIZ #4 *(from page 9)*

1. d
2. a
3. e
4. g
5. f
6. i
7. b
8. j
9. c
10. h

QUIZ #5 *(from page 11)*

1. True
2. False (It was on Saturday night.)
3. True
4. False (She was a singer.)
5. True
6. True
7. False (He hosted *Truth or Consequences*.)
8. True
9. False (*The Tonight Show With Johnny Carson*)
10. True

QUIZ #6   *(from page 13)*

1. He was a rabbi.
2. Marlo Thomas
3. Wayne and Schuster
4. Pat Buttram
5. I Married Joan
6. He worked in the sewer.
7. Gail Storm
8. "My Son, the Folk Singer"
9. Automobiles
10. Marie Wilson

QUIZ #7   *(from page 15)*

1. d
2. h
3. b
4. i
5. j
6. c
7. f
8. a
9. g
10. e

QUIZ #8   *(from page 17)*

1. Stan Laurel
2. Bride and Groom
3. Bye, Bye Birdie
4. Mary Poppins
5. Bert, the chimney sweeper
6. The Dick Van Dyke Show
7. Rob Petrie
8. Morey Amsterdam
9. Carl Reiner
10. Jerry

QUIZ #9   *(from page 19)*

1. i
2. b
3. g
4. e
5. d
6. c
7. j
8. h
9. a
10. f

QUIZ #10   *(from page 21)*

1. Laugh-In
2. Al, Harry, Jimmy
3. Russia
4. Eddie Lawrence
5. Groucho Marx
6. Piano
7. Don Ameche and Frances Langford
8. Norm Crosby
9. Sid Caesar
10. Merwyn Bogue

QUIZ #11   *(from page 23)*

1. f
2. d
3. g
4. i
5. c
6. h
7. e
8. j
9. a
10. b

QUIZ #12 *(from page 25)*

1. Mr. Warmth
2. Johnny Carson
3. Insult comedy
4. Jack E. Leonard
5. Dean Martin
6. The Tonight Show
7. "Hello, Dummy"
8. C.P.O. Sharkey
9. You, hockey puck
10. Bob Newhart

QUIZ #13 *(from page 27)*

1. c
2. a
3. h
4. d
5. e
6. b
7. i
8. g
9. f
10. j

QUIZ #14 *(from page 28)*

1. b
2. c
3. a
4. a & c
5. c
6. a
7. b
8. c
9. a
10. c

QUIZ #15   *(from page 29)*

1. e
2. f
3. i
4. a
5. b
6. d
7. g
8. c
9. j
10. h

QUIZ #16   *(from page 31)*

1. Andy Griffith
2. J. J.
3. W. C. Fields
4. Professor Backwards
5. Phil Silvers
6. Bergen/McCarthy Show
7. Steve Martin
8. Laugh-In
9. Edgar Kennedy
10. The Keystone Cops

QUIZ #17   *(from page 33)*

1. Uncle Milty
2. Charlie Chaplin
3. Sandra
4. Rudy Vallee
5. Philip Morris
6. Texaco Star Theater
7. The Buick-Berle Show
8. Tuesday
9. Sid Stone
10. Jimmy Nelson

QUIZ #18   *(from page 34)*

1. i
2. e
3. g
4. a
5. d
6. c
7. f
8. j
9. h
10. b

QUIZ #19   *(from page 35)*

1. Clarabell
2. My Friend Irma
3. Mel Blanc
4. Frank Fontaine
5. Johnny Carson
6. Robin Williams
7. Jerry Lester
8. Mr. Peepers
9. Billy Gilbert
10. Bob Burns

QUIZ #20   *(from page 37)*

1. e
2. j
3. g
4. b
5. a
6. d
7. i
8. h
9. c
10. f

QUIZ #21 *(from page 39)*

1. Ezra Stone
2. Spinach
3. Fibber McGee & Molly
4. Ed Wynn
5. Mel Blanc
6. Marie Wilson
7. Eddie Cantor
8. English
9. Mystic Knights of the Sea
10. Mary Livingstone

QUIZ #22 *(from page 41)*

1. Her grandmother
2. Lucille Ball
3. "I Made a Fool Of Myself Over John Foster Dulles"
4. Once Upon a Mattress
5. The Gary Moore Show
6. Twelve years
7. UCLA
8. Tarzan
9. Saying "hello" to her grandmother
10. Julie Andrews

QUIZ #23 *(from page 43)*

1. Penny Marshall and Cindy Williams
2. Joan Rivers
3. Totie Fields
4. Rose Nyland
5. *My Little Margie* and *Oh, Suzanna*
6. Las Vegas
7. Moms Mabley
8. Moms Mabley
9. Fanny Brice
10. The flute

QUIZ #24   *(from page 45)*

1. e
2. g
3. h
4. b
5. c
6. d
7. a
8. i
9. f
10. j

QUIZ #25   *(from page 47)*

RADIO:
Goodman Ace
Fanny Brice
Phil Harris – Alice Faye
Jack Pearl
Joe Penner

TELEVISION:
Redd Foxx
Don Adams
Dick Van Dyke
Bob Newhart
Carol Burnett

BOTH:
Milton Berle
Ed Wynn
Fred Allen
George Burns
Gertrude Berg

QUIZ #26   *(from page 49)*

1. Will Rogers
2. Milton Berle
3. A drunk
4. Trixie
5. Rodney Dangerfield
6. 700 Sundays
7. Red Buttons
8. Charlie Chaplin
9. Twenty years
10. The Color Purple

QUIZ #27   *(from page 51)*

1. d
2. h
3. e
4. b
5. c
6. g
7. a
8. i
9. f
10. j

QUIZ #28   *(from page 53)*

1. Henny
2. Henny
3. Henny
4. the violin
5. Morey
6. Morey
7. Henny
8. Henny
9. Morey
10. Morey

QUIZ #29 *(from page 55)*

1. d
2. a
3. f
4. h
5. g
6. c
7. e
8. j
9. b
10. i

QUIZ #30 *(from page 57)*

1. b
2. c
3. b
4. a
5. a
6. c
7. b
8. a
9. b
10. c

QUIZ #31 *(from page 59)*

1. h
2. j
3. e
4. d
5. i
6. g
7. f
8. b
9. c
10. a

QUIZ #32   *(from page 61)*
1. Ben Turpin
2. William Bendix
3. Martin and Lewis
4. Don Knotts
5. Fred Allen
6. All In the Family
7. Jim Nabors
8. The Sportsman Quartet
9. Pert Kelton
10. I've Got a Secret

QUIZ #33   *(from page 63)*
1. b
2. f
3. a
4. i
5. g
6. d
7. e
8. c
9. h
10. j

QUIZ #34   *(from page 64)*
1. Phyllis Diller
2. Our Miss Brooks
3. Lily Tomlin
4. Goldie Hawn
5. Judy Tenuta
6. Whoopie Goldberg
7. The Goldbergs
8. Bea Arthur
9. It Pays To Be Ignorant
10. The Little Rascals

QUIZ #35 *(from page 65)*

1. c
2. b
3. i
4. e
5. a
6. g
7. h
8. d
9. f
10. j

QUIZ #36 *(from page 67)*

1. True
2. True
3. False (She was the mother of the Marx Brothers.)
4. False (Lucky Strike)
5. True
6. False (Gilda Radner)
7. False (Joe E. Lewis)
8. True
9. False (He played the saxophone.)
10. False (Smith and Dale)

QUIZ #37 *(from page 69)*

1. Pat Harrington
2. George Carlin
3. Spanish
4. Steve Allen
5. Freeman Gosden and Charles Correll
6. Buster Keaton
7. Accounting
8. The Maxwell
9. Eugene
10. Joan Davis

QUIZ #38   *(from page 71)*

1. "The Great One"
2. He was a pool hustler.
3. The Life of Riley
4. Admiral Four Star Revue
5. Saturday
6. Ed Norton
7. Pert Kelton, Andrey Meadows, Sheila MacRae
8. He was a bus driver.
9. Crazy Guggenheim
10. Take Me Along

QUIZ #39   *(from page 72)*

1. f
2. e
3. i
4. d
5. j
6. c
7. h
8. b
9. g
10. a

QUIZ #40   *(from page 73)*

1. Bob Hope
2. The Breakfast Club
3. Higgins
4. Jimmy Durante
5. Joe 'em Down Store
6. Blanche and John
7. I Love a Mystery
8. The Judy Canova Show
9. Camel
10. The Bing Crosby Show

QUIZ #41 *(from page 75)*

1. b
2. c
3. a
4. b
5. a and b
6. c
7. a
8. c
9. All three
10. a

QUIZ #42 *(from page 77)*

1. Nathan Birnbaum
2. Gracie Allen
3. Pee Wee Quartette
4. She was a dancer.
5. Thirty-eight years
6. Maxwell House
7. The Happy Postman
8. Carnation
9. The Sunshine Boys
10. Jack Benny

QUIZ #43 *(from page 78)*

1. f
2. e
3. a
4. j
5. d
6. g
7. i
8. h
9. b
10. c

QUIZ #44   *(from page 79)*

1. Saturday Night Live
2. Denmark
3. Will Rogers
4. Clarinet
5. Our Gang
6. Popeye
7. Louis Nye
8. Leonard
9. Jan Murray
10. Fibber McGee and Molly

QUIZ #45   *(from page 81)*

1. e
2. g
3. j
4. h
5. f
6. a
7. i
8. b
9. c
10. d

QUIZ #46   *(from page 82)*

1. I've Got a Secret
2. Ernestine
3. Tony Randall and Jack Klugman
4. Ernie Kovacs
5. Tom and Dick
6. Dayton Allen
7. Cosmo
8. Mr. Peepers
9. Chris Elliott
10. David Letterman

QUIZ #47 *(from page 83)*

1. j
2. i
3. b
4. d
5. c
6. e
7. g
8. a
9. h
10. f

QUIZ #48 *(from page 85)*

1. Philadelphia
2. Temple University
3. Track and Field
4. Shoe maker
5. Jack Paar
6. I Spy
7. Fat Albert
8. The Cosby Show
9. Cliff Huxtable
10. Six

QUIZ #49 *(from page 87)*

1. i
2. f
3. g
4. a
5. e
6. j
7. c
8. d
9. h
10. b

QUIZ #50   *(from page 89)*

1. Mrs. Calabash
2. Saturday
3. Jane
4. Fred Allen
5. Rip Taylor
6. Bob Hope
7. They both played The Great Gildersleeve
8. Edgar Kennedy
9. Alan King
10. Halfway up the hill

QUIZ #51   *(from page 91)*

1. g
2. e
3. d
4. f
5. b
6. h
7. j
8. c
9. a
10. i

QUIZ #52   *(from page 93)*

1. Julliard
2. Saxophone
3. Admiral Four Star Revue
4. Your Show of Shows
5. Max Leibman
6. Saturday
7. Imogene Coca
8. Caesar's Hour
9. Nanette Fabray
10. Edie Adams

QUIZ #53 *(from page 94)*

1. True
2. True
3. False (Who's On First?)
4. True
5. False (Played by Ruth Buzzi)
6. True
7. True (She was his wife.)
8. False
9. True
10. True

QUIZ #54 *(from page 95)*

1. Robin Williams
2. "Hello Mudduh, Hello Fadduh"
3. Bob Hope
4. The Old Philosopher
5. Who's On First?
6. Artie Johnson
7. Mitch Dewood and Steve Rossi
8. Jim Nabors
9. Paul Lynde
10. W. C. Fields

QUIZ #55 *(from page 97)*

1. Amos Jacobs
2. Burns and Allen
3. The Jazz Singer
4. Marlo
5. Phil Donahue
6. Make Room For Daddy
7. Twelve years
8. Rusty
9. Uncle Tonoose
10. St. Jude Children's Research Hospital

QUIZ #56   *(from page 99)*
1. b
2. b
3. c
4. a
5. c
6. a
7. c
8. b
9. a
10. b

QUIZ #57   *(from page 101)*
1. Burt Lahr
2. The Bowery Boys
3. Vaughn Meader
4. Jonathan Winters
5. Twenty-two years
6. The Fish
7. Carl Reiner
8. Baby Snooks
9. David and Ricky
10. Mort Sahl

QUIZ #58   *(from page 103)*
1. Red
2. My Favorite Husband
3. Richard Denning
4. 1951-1957
5. The Lucy Show
6. Here's Lucy
7. Desi Arnaz
8. Lucy Ricardo
9. Wildcat
10. Mame

QUIZ #59   *(from page 105)*

1. e
2. i
3. j
4. h
5. f
6. g
7. b
8. a
9. c
10. d

QUIZ #60   *(from page 107)*

1. Gene Wilder
2. Mel Brooks
3. Smith and Dale
4. Irwin Corey
5. Mae Questel
6. Meathead
7. Johnny Carson
8. Sophie Tucker
9. Mickey Rooney
10. "The Chinese Waiter"

www.ingramcontent.com/pod-product-compliance
Lightning Source LLC
Chambersburg PA
CBHW070925270326
41927CB00011B/2732